Nonprofit Accounting & Financial Statements

Bookkeeping for Churches and Small Businesses

Tim Jefferson

Copyright © 2019

Dedicated to all my readers

Table of Contents

INTRODUCTION 7

1 8

THE BASICS OF ACCOUNTING FOR NONPROFITS 8

What really is a nonprofit organization? 9

General Duties o f a Bookkeeper 10

How long should your organization keep all its financials documents? 20

2 22

ACCOUNTING FOR CASH AND NON CASH DONATIONS 22

Steps for accounting for stock donations 23

Tracking donors 24

3 26

HOW TO ACCOUNT FOR NONPROFITS 26

Contents of the financial reports of nonprofits 26

Accounting procedures for nonprofits 27

Key steps for accounting for nonprofits 28

Fund accounting 33

4 34

ACCOUNTING FOR CHURCHES 34

Treatment of asset donations 34

5 40

ACCOUNTING FOR CLUBS 40

6 52

CHALLENGES IN ACCOUNTING FOR NONPROFITS 52

Reasons why nonprofits have problems with their accounting 53

7 55

PREVENTING COMMON NONPROFIT ACCOUNTING CHALLENGES 55

How to resolve nonprofits accounting problems 55

8 59

WHY GRANTS PROPOSALS GET REJECTED 59

How to improve grant writing skills 59

Tips for writing simple, readable proposals 62

9 64

EFFICIENT NONPROFIT ACCOUNTING SOFTWARE 64

10 66

PICTURES OF FINANCIAL STATEMENTS OF NONPROFITS 66

11 75

NONPROFIT ACCOUNTING GLOSSARY 75

ABOUT THE AUTHOR 83

INTRODUCTION

This book was designed to help both Accountants and non-Accountants handle all matters relating to Accounting and Finance for nonprofit organizations.

Clubs, Societies, and Churches will find this book especially useful as it provides the basic information needed for keeping a list of income and expenses, collecting and distributing funds, reconciling bank statements every month to ensure it includes checks and other third party payment gateways, budgeting events that the nonprofit shall host, preparing treasurer's reports, and preparing and filing annual tax return for the organization (if applicable).

All questions, comments and suggestions should be directed to the author by visiting the page Nonprofit Finance on Facebook.

1

THE BASICS OF ACCOUNTING FOR NONPROFITS

There are only two types of organizations that can be run. For-profit and nonprofit organization. So, while some organizations are set up to make and distribute profits among members, others are set up to carry on objects calculated to improve the welfare of members socially, educationally, spiritually and so on. This kind of organization is referred to as a nonprofit. As a consultant, I offer practical financial advisory services to both organizations. And you know what, organizations set up for profit-making are tougher to handle. Auditors will always acknowledge window dressing in accounting books and other forms of accounting malpractices when handling organizations set up for profit. But then, our concern, the reason you bought this book, is how you can learn to account for nonprofit organizations. These organizations include friendly societies, clubs, churches and associations etc.

If you run a nonprofit organization, you'll realize that tax payments, recordkeeping, and financial statements are handled differently than other businesses. That leads to the question; what really is a nonprofit organization?

What really is a nonprofit organization?

In June 2015, Michele Brown, my childhood friend (currently lives in Africa) started up an NGO that specializes in providing support to Educationally Disadvantaged children in Congo. This is a type of nonprofit organization. These organizations operate to fulfill a scientific, educational, religious or charitable purpose. Even though nonprofits need finance to operate, making profit isn't the essence of their existence.

Many nonprofits aren't being taxed. Once they are deemed qualified for a tax-exempt status, they aren't mandated to federal business income taxes. However, they are not exempted from paying state and local income taxes. Keep in mind too, that not all nonprofits are tax-exempt. For your organization to qualify for exemption, it has to be classified under 501 (c) (3) organizations.

Sadly, funds in nonprofits are mismanaged most of the time. As a result of weak accounting system, fraud and theft have become very common. It becomes relevant for someone with experience to handle the books of accounts of a nonprofit. But if you have been bestowed with the task of managing the books of your club or church and you have no prior knowledge of bookkeeping, just smile. Yes you should smile because this book will provide you a guide on what to do.

If you are new in the business of bookkeeping why not ask for prior documents, the duties you are responsible for, the accounting software used by the nonprofit, and the funds available to the organization. But what will be the general duties of a treasurer or bookkeeper? The following subheading provides an insight.

General Duties o f a Bookkeeper

- To keep a list of income and expenses for the nonprofit.
- To collect and distribute funds in behalf of the nonprofit.
- To reconcile bank statements every month to ensure it includes checks and other third party payment gateways
- To budget events that the nonprofit shall host.
- To prepare treasurer's reports.
- To prepare and file annual tax return for the club (if applicable).

To keep a list of all income and expenses for the nonprofit

As a bookkeeper, there are two key things you should always do regarding income and expenses. You should endeavor to keep **copies** and make **notes**. This may seem too simple, but it may be easily overlooked. Always take notes and keep copies because you will need to look back for information regarding cost of items sold and how much was paid to the organization. You might also need to prove your organization's annual tax return information to the IRS.

A very good place to store documents will be an online file storage system like Google Drive. It is easily accessible and can help group your documents in one place.

Now that you are able to store your club's documents, you will need to manage the numbers. Does your organization use accounting software? And if not, is there a need to start using one? Intuit QuickBooks are a great option. Though the software will greatly help organize a lot of your bookkeeping needs for your organization, it is expensive and a bit difficult to learn. If you are not familiar with accounting software then you are likely to make a lot of mistakes without even knowing .if your nonprofit organization has been operating without accounting software, you might as well just relax and flow with them.

To collect and distribute funds on behalf of the nonprofit

The major responsibility of any bookkeeper is to ensure he receives and distributes money in behalf of the nonprofit. In clear terms, this will be your income and expenses.

Income isn't any difficult to understand. It includes membership dues fundraisers, event attendance etc. Expenses on the other hand includes paying for food and drink for meeting events, incurring annual state registration obligations etc.

Payments can be made using checks, online bill payment options or with a debit/credit card. If your organization is small it may not have set up any of these methods of payment. With cash becomes the payment means. The problem with making payments through cash only is that it will make tracking your money for the club difficult. If your nonprofit is using this method, it's important to keep detailed documentation of the money spent and received in behalf of the club and society or church.

Reconcile bank statements every month to ensure it includes checks and any third party payment gateways

Expenses:

It is necessary to group expense according to type. This will help you keep transactions of a similar nature together so you can have just one total for that category. Whenever you are trying to track how much is being spent on items, you will likely find recurring transactions. Are there items that are purchased multiple times every month? You should group the transactions together according to type to determine how much was spent in total each month on all the items.

For example, if your organization is hosting a few events at the end of the year and your board has had flyers printed out to give to local pet stores for promotion, and gone to the grocery store and purchased food and drink to sell at the event, you would need to record these purchases on a spreadsheet or in your accounting software and apply them to the account (or category) that best describes what they are for. Normally, the flyers would be grouped under 'printing'. The food and drink would be under "Food and Entertainment"

The point here is to use a moderate number of accounts to correctly sort out your organization's expenses. If you notice your account categories have become too much, try to work on them for clarity and clean presentation else the purpose of organizing your expenses in an easy to view format has been defeated.

Income:

If you are just starting, you will likely need just one category for income. But as soon as your organization starts holding events, you will have to add a few new categories to help split out where you are generating income from.

For example, your nonprofit is organizing a scholarship program. You will need to separate donations for these particular programs in your categories from your other income groupings. A corresponding expense account will also need to be set up to coincide with the program income for payments that your nonprofit will issue such as "scholarships awarded".

Does your club have a bank account?

I expect that your nonprofit has a bank account already. But if it doesn't, keep in mind that it's going to open an account in the organization's name. the documents you will likely need includes (but not limited to) a Federal ID number issued by the IRS, state corporation commission documents proving the existence of the organization at the state level, and details of those who will have access to the account. If your organization has been issued a Non-Profit status, then you may have to come along with that documentation. Access to the account should be granted to no more than three individuals.

If the organization already has a bank account set up, fine. You only need to keep track of and reconcile the monthly bank statements. This will help for proper accounting for your nonprofit. You will be able to determine if there are discrepancies in the account and keep track of your income and expenses.

Creating a Profit and Loss Statement

A profit and loss statement can be used in many aspects of your organization finances. It is easy to set up and will help you determine net profit. Net profit or loss is determined by subtracting your expenses from your total revenue. You will have either a profit or a loss. If you have a loss on your statement, which is a negative number, then it's time you pay attention to what your income and expense issues are. This report will help you pinpoint where you may be spending too much, and tackle the issues.

SAMPLE CLUB PROFIT & LOSS STATEMENT

	Total
Revenue	
Memberships	$ 250.00
Raffle	500.00
Meeting Tickets	500.00
Gross Profit	$ 1,250.00
Expenditures	
Advertising	$ -0-
Bank Charges	0.00
Computers	0.00
Food & Entertainment	750.00
Dues & Subscriptions	35.00
Office Expenses	10.00
Postage/Shipping	1.00
Printing	200.00
Uniforms	100.00
Misc.	0.00
Total Expenditures	1,096.00
Net Profit (Loss)	$ 154.00

Source: masma.org

Learn to budget events and special occasions that the nonprofit shall host

A budget for your organization is not different from the one you use to track personal income and expenses at home. You are trying to project what your income and expenses will be in the next month or so. Remember to budget reasonably. You have to critically look at all your income and expenses, and ask tough questions. Is there a possibility of more or less members renewing in the following year? If you are holding another event, has the venue changed or has the rent fee soared? Has the cost of office supplies soared or will there be a need for more supplies in the following year?

There are lots of factors to consider when making estimates. Budgeting takes practice to get things sorted out. The god thing is that when you finally know your onions, you will have several years' worth of numbers to help you better able to average your costs.

SAMPLE CLUB BUDGET

	2016	Projected
Revenue		
Meeting Tickets	$ 250.00	$ 300.00
Raffle	500.00	700.00
Gross Profit	$ 750.00	$ 1,000.00
Expenditures		
Advertising	$ 25.00	$ 50.00
Decorations	15.00	20.00
Food & Beverage	50.00	75.00
Printing	10.00	10.00
Raffle Prizes	100.00	125.00
Raffle Tickets	5.00	5.00
Venue	100.00	100.00
Wrist Bands	5.00	5.00
Misc.	100.00	100.00
Total Expenditures	410.00	490.00
Net Profit (Loss)	$ 340.00	$ 510.00

Source: masma.org

Treasurer's Report

A treasurer's report provides members an idea of the organization's finances. A good treasurer's report should include a current cash balance for all accounts of the organization, current outstanding expenses, and anticipated future expenses. Any expected future revenue, should be captured, and should close with an estimated ending balance.

Treasurer's Report
Public Board Meeting
May 1, 2017

CASH		
Acme Bank		$ 2,000.00
Paypal		500.00
TOTAL		$ 2,500.00
EXPENSES		
Checks/Payments Issued		$ 25.00
Checks/Payments estimated		100.00
SUB TOTAL		$ 125.00
RECEIVABLES		
Memberships		$ 100.00
TOTAL		$ 100.00
ENDING CASH BALANCE		$ 2,475.00

Source: masma.org

Filing your organization's annual tax return

A nonprofit is required to file an annual income tax return to the government. In most cases, the organization is small enough that a form 990N (or 990 Postcard) is all that is needed. It is for clubs with $50,000 or less in total revenue for the year.

If your nonprofit has over $50,000 a year for three consecutive years, then a Form 990EZ will need to be filed. It is best that you hire a paid tax specialist who's knowledgeable of non-profit tax returns in order to prepare the return.

How long should your organization keep all its financials documents?

The IRS has guidelines regarding how long financial records should be kept. But it is advisable to apply caution. The beauty of using an online file storage provider like Google Drive is the plenty of space you have for storing documents for as long as possible.

Documents to keep permanently

- Your Corporate Records and By-Laws
- Federal ID Documentation – issued by the IRS.
- Federal and state tax return.
- State Corporation Commission documents – the Secretary of your organization should be responsible for this.
- Chart of Accounts–these are your categories you set up for your cash disbursement sheet
- Back up copy of your bookkeeping software or cash disbursement sheets.
- Federal and/or state information returns
- Interim & Year End Financial statements

Documents to keep for up to seven years

- Your Bank statements and reconciliations
- Your paid bills and receipts
- Petty cash vouchers (if applicable)
- Your cash receipts and disbursements
- Your invoices to customers

2

ACCOUNTING FOR CASH AND NON CASH DONATIONS

It is quite common for nonprofits to receive donations of stock, especially at year end as this helps donors to give to nonprofits in such a way that fits into their overall personal tax planning. Most organizations have a gift policy requiring that gifts of stock are liquidated once received to minimize the risk associated with the stock market.

Ordinarily, when your nonprofit receives a stock donation, a thank you letter should be sent to the donor. The letter should acknowledge the gift of stock, such as the name and number of shares. The value of the stock should not be listed since the organization is not in the business of valuing stock. In accordance with the Generally Accepted Accounting Principles (GAAP), once stock is received from a donor, a contribution should be recorded at the fair value of the stock on the date received. If the fair value of the stock upon receipt is greater than the pledge receivable balance, the organization should record a contribution for the difference.

If your nonprofit's policy is to sell stock immediately, any difference between the proceeds received from the sale of stock and the fair value recorded on the date the stock was received will be recorded as a realized gain or loss on the books. Any fees incurred while selling the stock should be recorded as investment fees expense.

It is needful to say that non cash donations can be tangible (furniture, stock, supplies, clothing, equipment, etc.) or intangible (accounting, legal, maintenance, etc.). These donations should be recorded as in-kind contributions.

Cash donations are counted as income on the financial statement.

Steps for accounting for stock donations

The following steps will help you to account for donated assets.

- Understand what fair market value really means
- Record a transaction if assets are simply passed to another organization.
- Determine whether the transaction is a contribution or an exchange
- Research the market to determine the exit price.
- Estimate a fair market value
- Value the asset using a donor-supplied price

Keep in mind that donations should be recorded in the organization's general ledger. Once that has been done, donations are then recorded in the organization's transaction journal. The value of the donation should be listed as an asset in the debits column of the journal. It is then listed as a credit for the same amount in the credits column.

Tracking donors

Keeping a thorough and accurate accounting of donors helps nonprofits track who's donating to them. Every donor should be placed into a database listing names, addresses, contact information, and value and frequency of donations.

3

HOW TO ACCOUNT FOR NONPROFITS

Whether you are about starting a nonprofit or already have one, you'll benefit a great deal from understanding the unique aspects of accounting for a nonprofit organization. I'll explain the aspects one-by-one. They are quite easy to understand. Are you ready?

Contents of the financial reports of nonprofits

The financial report of a nonprofit often includes the following:

I. Receipts and Payments Account
II. Income and Expenditure Account
III. Balance Sheet

It is good to keep in mind that the following differences in terminology;

While **Capital** is the sum owed by a business (or for profit organization), **Accumulated Fund** is the sum owed by the nonprofit to its members.

For a nonprofit, **Surplus Fund** is the excess of income over expenditure. Such excess is referred to as **Profit** in a for profit organization.

Deficit is the excess of expenditure over income in a nonprofit, while **Loss** is the excess of expenditure over income in a business organization.

Accounting procedures for nonprofits

No matter the type of nonprofit you run, the following accounting procedures can never be sidelined:

I. Preparation of opening statement of affairs in order to arrive at the accumulated fund (this is done if the statement of affairs had not been prepared previously. If the statement had been prepared, move to the next step.

II. Preparation of a summary of receipts and payments for the period.
III. Updating the ledger accounts to include transactions that took place during the accounting period, plus certain adjustments on the Income and Expenditure A/C. the adjustments include depreciation of assets, prepayments and accruals etc.
IV. Preparation of a Trial Balance to check the arithmetical accuracy of ledger entries.
V. Preparation of Income and Expenditure Account to ascertain the deficit or the net surplus for the period.
VI. Preparation of Balance Sheet to show the financial position of the nonprofit.

Key steps for accounting for nonprofits

In order to fully take charge of the books of account of your nonprofit, you should keep the following steps in mind:

Choose an accounting method

Nonprofit bookkeeping relies strongly on selecting a method for recording your income and expenses (you might choose to say incoming and outgoing money). Like any business, your nonprofit needs finance to absorb operating expenses. You'll need money to pay utility bills, rent, employee wages, and so on. All sources of income and expenditure outlay must be recorded with an organized accounting system. Now, you can chose to take the records in any of the two the following two accounting systems.

Cash-basis accounting: in this system, expenses and incomes are being recorded as soon as they are paid or received, not when the transaction took place. I'll explain further. If you run a nonprofit, for example, where members are required to pay dues, using the cash-basis system, records of payments will only be taken when the members pay. However, this system will not work for you if you make an annual gross sale of more than $5 million or more than $1 million in gross receipts for inventory sales, or if you extend credit facilities.

Accrual accounting: in this system, transactions are recorded when they take place and not when money is received or paid for them. Using the example of membership dues, you'll need to take record of income once you send invoice to members, even though physical cash is yet to be received.

Create the proper financial statements

An appropriate financial statement will boost accounting efficiency. You need one to correctly record your organization's finances. The financial statements are classified into three (3)

- Balance sheets (statement of financial position)
- Income statements
- Cash flow statements

You will never be able to do without the above three. The statement of financial position is especially key. It gives you an overview of the financial health of your nonprofit during a period of time. This statement shows the assets, liabilities, and net assets (equity). The addition of net assets or equity and liabilities must be the same with the assets on the statement of financial position.

STATEMENT OF FINANCIAL POSITION		
JANUARY 31, 2018		
ASSETS		**LIABILITIES & NET ASSETS**
Cash & Cash Equivalents	$46,000	Liabilities $1,000
		Net Assets
		With Donor Restrictions $30,000
		Without Donor Restrictions $15,000
Total Assets	**$46,000**	**Total Liabilities & Net Assets $46,000**

While recording net assets, endeavor to classify them. They can be classified as 'with donor restrictions' or 'without donor retractions'. This is necessary because some donors might state the specific reason for their donations. When this is the case, donations should be recorded under 'with donor restrictions'.

The income statement is especially useful for recording revenue and expenses during a period of time. Like the statement of financial position, revenues should be recorded with or without restrictions.

STATEMENT OF ACTIVITIES
FOR THE MONTH ENDED DECEMBER 31, 2018

	Without Donor Restrictions	With Donor Restrictions	Total
Revenues			
Donor Contributions	$5,000	$20,000	$25,000
Membership Dues	$10,000	—	$10,000
	$15,000	$20,000	$35,000
Expenses			
Wages	$8,000	—	$8,000
Change in Net Assets	$7,000	$20,000	$27,000
Net Assets-Beginning	—	—	—
Net Assets-Ending	$7,000	$20,000	$27,000

Finally, the cash flow statement shows how money enters and leaves your organization during a specific period of time. The cash flow statement organizes cash movement into three categories, which are operating, investing, and financing activities. Your organization can have either positive or negative cash flow.

CASH FLOW STATEMENT
FOR THE YEAR ENDED DECEMBER 2018

Operating Activities	
Net Income	$10,000
Investing Activities	
Cash Paid for Equipment	($5,000)
Financing Activities	
Net Increase in Cash	$5,000

Fund accounting

Fund accounting basically describes how nonprofits track and separate their expenses from revenues. Nonprofits need to understand fund accounting because it allows them to clearly see how donor money is being used. As your organization spends donor money, you'll be able to see how much of it is restricted vs. unrestricted. Both classes of donations must be entered in your accounting software in such a way that it can be tracked so you easily see how much is left of a particular restricted account.

4

ACCOUNTING FOR CHURCHES

You may be reading this book because you are the bookkeeper of your church. If that is the case, pay careful attention to every detail in this chapter. Accounting for churches isn't really very complex. The records are straight-forward. However, you may frequently receive asset donations. How do you treat asset donations?

Treatment of asset donations

When fixed assets are donated to the church take the following actions;

DR Fixed Assets Account (concerned)

CR: Capital Donation Account

At the end of the year, the balance on Capital Donation Account must be written off to the Income and Expenditure Account.

Now, we are going to use a hypothetical scenario to explain how to account for a church.

The Scenario

Judge is in charge of managing the accounting records for an Apostolic Church in the U.S. Monies collected from members of the church must be brought together and summarized in a **Receipts and Payments account**. He has the following information for the year ended 20x9.

	$
Free-Will Offerings	3,980
Collections	5,000
Harvest Levies Received	2,960
Annual Dues Received	9,800
Salaries of:	
-Full-time Pastors	4,000
-Secretary	2,600
-Watchmen	1,000
Commission on sales of Gospel Journals	200
Electricity	100

Thanksgiving Donation	8,980
Auditorium Decoration	1,700
Repairs/Maintenance of equipment	1,600
Printing & Stationery	3,000
Construction of toilets	10,000
Telephone and Postage	1,000
New chairs	2,500
New musical instrument	2,000
7 Wall Clocks-donation	500
Environmental Decorations	1,500
Unclaimed cash, lost but found on convention field	100
Harvest Offerings	4,900
Rental income from musical instruments	4,000
Auditorium Expansion n Appeal Fund	60,000
Opening balance	11,800

Judge is required to prepare a receipts and Payments account for the year ended 31st December 20x9. How can this be done? Consider the following solution.

THE APOSTOLIC CHURCH OF NIGERIA

RECEIPTS AND PAYMENTS ACCOUNT FOR THE YEAR ENDED 31ST DECEMBER 20X9

	$		$	$
Balance b/d	11,000	Salaries:		
Offerings	5,000	-Pastors	4,000	
Free-will offerings	3,980	-Secretary	2,600	
Harvest Levies	2,960	Watchmen	1,000	7,600
Annual Dues	9,800	Decoration of Auditorium		1,700
Commission on sales		Printing & Sta.		3,000
Of Gospel Journals	200	Electricity		100
Lost but found money	100	Telephone & Postage		1,100
Thanksgiving Donations	8,980	Construction of Toilets		10,000
Rental income from		Rep. & Maintenance of		
Musical instruments	4,000	Equipment		1,600
Harvest Offerings	4,900	New musical instruments		2,000
Auditorium Expansion		New Chairs (furniture)		2,500
Appeal Fund	60,000	Environmental Decorations		1,500
		Balance c/d		31,100
	110,920			110,920

Notes on the Account

The donation of 7 wall clocks was $500. This figure isn't included in the Receipts and Payments account since it is not a cash item. It is a capital donation.

The balance of includes the lost but found sum of $100. The sum is held in custody for the owner.

The first solution is a T-format presentation. On the next page, we are going to adopt a vertical format presentation in solving the problem.

VERTICAL PRESENTATION

THE APOSTOLIC CHURCH OF NIGERIA
RECEIPTS AND PAYMENTS ACCOUNT FOR THE YEAR ENDED 31ST DECEMBER 20X9

	$	$
Balance b/d		11,000
Receipts for the year:		
Offerings		5,000
Free-will offerings		3,980
Harvest Levies		2,960
Annual Dues		9,800
Commission on sales Of Gospel Journals		200
Lost but found money		100
Thanksgiving Donations		8,980
Rental income from musical instruments		4,000
Harvest Offerings		4,900
Auditorium Expansion appeal Fund		60,000
		110,920
Payments for the year:		
Salaries –		
-Pastors	4,000	
-Secretary	2,600	
-Watchmen	1,000	7,600
Decoration of Auditorium		1,700
Printing & Stationary		3,000
Electricity		100
Telephone & Postage		1,100
Construction of Toilets		10,000
Repairs & Maintenance of equipment		1,600
New musical instruments		2,000
New Chairs (furniture)		2,500
Environmental Decorations		1,500
Balance c/d		31,100
		110,920

5

ACCOUNTING FOR CLUBS

The accounts of clubs (including associations and friendly societies) are very similar to accounts of churches. However, complexity arises regarding subscription, an annual dues payable by members. Some members pay a lump sum for the rest of their lifetime in lieu of the usual yearly subscriptions. Such money must be recognized in the Income and Expenditure Account for an estimated number of years based on the accounting policy of the nonprofit.

The accounting treatment for such payment is straightforward. When such money is received, Bank Account is debited, while Life Membership Account is credited. At the end of every year, the Life Membership Account is debited, while Income and Expenditure Account is credited.

In the example below, Michael is in charge of handling the books of Account of X & Y Club. He needs to prepare Income and Expenditure account, and Balance sheet as at

31st December 20x9. The following information relates to the club:

	$
Accumulated Fund on the last balance Sheet	187,200
Annual Subscription	67,400
Printing and Stationery	35,300
Furniture and Fittings (Cost)	70,000
Office Equipment (Cost)	28,500
Sundry Incomes	18,400
Entertainment Costs	7,100
Office rent and rates	12,300
Annual Government grants	21,500
Cash in hand	2,600
Bank balance	22,300
Cash on Deposit at 5% pa	50,480
Profit on sales of uniforms	9,900
Staff salaries	40,500
Entrance fees	21,400
Repairs and Maintenance of Equipment	18,300

Annual fund-raising collections	22,400
Sundry Creditors	16,200
Rent received	4,500
Audit fees	2,000
Dividend received	600
Interest on bank deposit	2,400
Land (for headquarters building)	44,900
Annual General Meeting expenses	6,600
General expenses	5,700
Stocks of uniforms and other valuables	25,500

Depreciate furniture and office equipment at 10% per annum on cost. $1,900 out of the subscription is paid in advance by members and $1,100 is in arrears. $1,600 is owing for staff salaries.

Solution to the problem

X AND Y CLUB

INCOME AND EXPENDITURE ACCOUNT FR THE YEAR ENDED 31ST DECEMBER 20X9

INCOME	$
Sundry Incomes	18,400
Annual government grants	21,500
Profit on sales of uniforms	9,900
Entrance fees	21,400
Annual fund-raising collection	22,400
Rent received	4,500
Dividend received	600
Interest on bank deposit	2,400
Subscription (2)	66,600
Total income	167700

EXPENDITURE	$
Printing & Stationery	35,300
Environmental Costs	7,100

Office rent & rates	12,300	
Repairs & Maintenance of Equip.	18,300	
Audit fees	2,000	
Annual general meeting expenses	6,600	
General expenses	5,700	
Depreciation: (1) Furniture	6,910	
Equipment	2,760	
Staff Salaries (3)	42,100	
Total Expenditure		(139.070)
Surplus funds for the year		28,630
Accumulated Funds b/f		187,200
Accumulated Fund c/f		215,830

X AND Y CLUB

BALANCE SHEET AS AT 31ST DECEMBER 20X9

REPRESENTED BY:	COST	DEPN	NBV
FIXED ASSETS	$	$	$
Land	44,900	-	44,900
Furniture & Fittings	70,000	(7,000)	63,000
Office Equipment	28,500	(2,850)	25,650
	143,400	9,850	133,550
CURRENT ASSETS			
Stock off uniforms etc.	25,500		
Cash on deposit at 5%	50,480		
Bank	22,300		
Cash in hand subscription	2,600		
Subscription in arrears	1,100		
Total Current Assets		101,980	
LESS: CURRENT LIABILITIES			
Sundry Creditors	16,200		
Subscription in advance	1,900		
Accrued salaries	1,600		

Total Current Liabilities	(19,700)	
Excess of Current Assets over Current Liabilities		82,200
		215,830
FINANCED BY		
Accumulated Funds		215,630

NOTES ON THE ACCOUNT

1(a) Depreciation of Assets:

Furniture & Fittings $\dfrac{10}{100} \times 70,000 = 7,000$

(b) Equipment: $\dfrac{10}{100} \times 28,500 = 2,850$

2 Subscription A/c

	$		$
Balance b/d	-	Bank	67,400
Income & Expenditure	66,600		
Subscription in advance	1,900	Subscription in arrears c/d	1,100
	68,500		68,500
Subscription in arrears b/d	1,100	subscription in advance b/d	1,900

3   Staff Salaries A/c

	$		$
Bank	40,500	Income & expenditure	42,100
Balance (owing)	1,600		
	42,100		42,100
		Balance owing b/d	1,600

Scenario 2

Kasmine Association club treasurer, keeps an analyzed cash book and presents the following vertical summary of receipts and payments on 31 October 2005

Opening Bank Balances

1 November 2004

Deposit account	2379
Current account	1680
	4059

Receipts for year:

Rents	7660
Bank interest	25
Members subscriptions	500
	12244

Payments for year:

Wages	410
Accountancy fees	75
Water rates	2260
Council rent	3100
Fencing repairs	35
Stationery	15
Sundries	90
Allotment prize	50
Adverts	20
Removal of rubbish	55
Skip hire	75
New strimmer	420
	6605

Bank Balances

31 October 2005

Deposit account	4139
Current account	1500
	5639

You are supplied with the following additional information:

a. On 1 November 2004 the club owned premises that were valued at £10500. Although these should be depreciated, the club has decided not to make such provisions.
b. At the beginning of the period it owned machinery and equipment that were worth £5100. It also acquired new machinery during the year valued at £420.
c. It depreciates such assets at 10% per annum on their Net Book Value.
d. At the beginning of the year they were owed £75 in late subscriptions and £55 were outstanding for the current year at 31 October 2005.
e. The club owed £45 at the end of the year for skip hire. It further owed water rates of £190 and council rent of £260 on 31 October 2005
f. From the above information you are required to prepare Income and Expenditure Account for the year and a Balance Sheet as at 31 October 2005.

Balance Sheet as at 31 October 2005

		£
Fixed Assets (NBV)		
Premises		10500
Equipment		4968
		15468
Current Assets		
Current account	1500	
Deposit account	4139	
Subscriptions due, unpaid	55	
	5694	
Less Current Liabilities		
Creditors	495	
Net Current Assets		5199
Total Assets Less Current Liabilities		**£20667**

Financed By:

	£
Accumulated Fund:	
1 November 2004	19734
Add excess income over expenditure for year	933
	£20667

Working Papers:

- Accumulated Fund as at 1 November 2004

Assets:	£
Premises	10500
Machinery	5100
Bank	4059
Subscriptions in arrears	75
	£19734

- Subscriptions

Subscriptions Account

2004	Balance b/d	75	2004	Bank	500
2005	I & E a/c	480		Subs due Unpaid Balance c/d	55
		£555			£555

- Water Rates and Council Rents

Rents and Rates a/c

2005	Bank	2260	2005	I & E a/c (Rates)	2450
2005	Bank	3100	2005	I & E a/c (Rents)	3360
2005	Balance c/d (Rates due)	190			
2005	Balance c/d (Rents due)	260			
		£5810			£5810
			2005	Balances b/d	450

- Skip Hire

Skip Hire Account

2005	Bank	75	2005	I & E a/c	120
2005	Balance c/d (due unpaid)	45			
		£120			£120
			2005	Balance b/d	45

- Fixed Asset Schedule

Fixed Assets	Premises £	Machinery £	Total £
Balance at 1 November 2004	10500	5100	15600
Additions in year		420	420
	10500	5520	16020
Less depreciation for year		552	552
Net Book Value at 31 October 2005	£10500	£4968	£15468

6

CHALLENGES IN ACCOUNTING FOR NONPROFITS

Nonprofits have to comply with many accounting rules and regulations, thus making their accounting tasks a bit challenging. Having worked with a handful of nonprofits over the years, I understand the challenges firsthand. But with the help of nonprofit accounting software, nonprofits can resolve these bottlenecks. They include:

1. Grant Tracking:

Nonprofits get grants from various sources, and it can be challenging to keep track of when and how often money is to be collected. It becomes necessary to use grant management software to keep track of grants movement.

2. Cash Flow Management:

Efficient and effective management of cash flow is necessary for nonprofits. There is Accounting software that can help keep everyone informed of the cash flow situation with its ability to create reports.

3. Managing Payroll:

People want to get their wages and salaries as soon as possible. As a result, nonprofits must learn to implement payroll themselves or hire someone to do it for them. There are some nonprofit accounting software solutions that come with payroll modules, thus making the payroll process seamless.

Reasons why nonprofits have problems with their accounting

Many nonprofits have problems with their accounting and financial reporting. These problems manifest themselves in financial reporting that is often inaccurate, late, or not available at all. This issue must be addressed by the nonprofit sector. Most of the data that boards and executive directors rely on to run nonprofits come from their accounting departments. Data that come in late, erroneous, or nonexistent will have a deleterious effect on decision-making

The following are reasons why nonprofits have problems with their accounting:

- Accounting rules for nonprofits are more complicated to understand and to apply than for-profit accounting rules.
- Nonprofits have a remarkable propensity for hiring people who do not know accounting to do their accounting.
- There is greater demand for financial data in a nonprofit, so expectations of your accounting department are greater. Data needs to be provided regularly to donors, funders, contributors, lenders, and government agencies.

7

PREVENTING COMMON NONPROFIT ACCOUNTING CHALLENGES

A study done by Dr. Jeffrey Burks , Deloitte Faculty Fellow and associate professor of accountancy, University of Notre Dame, showed that nonprofits have a 6.1 percent accounting error rate—roughly 60 percent higher than the error rate for publicly traded corporations. The study father found that 71 percent of nonprofit accounting errors are the products of bookkeeping and recording errors.

How to resolve nonprofits accounting problems

Do not rely on volunteers or untrained personnel

One reason financial mismanagement is a common setback for nonprofits is that untrained volunteers are expected to manage and perform recordkeeping and accounting activities. This expectation can lead to inaccurate recording of transactions, which results in poor financial report.

Employ a Professional Bookkeeper or Accountant

Most nonprofits delegate recordkeeping to untrained personnel for reasons pertaining to funding. Many nonprofits operate on shoestring budgets. They want to cut down cost.

It is true that many accounting software programs can help a person to input cash receipt activity quite easily, but what these software programs cannot replace is an experienced person's skill.

If your nonprofit that can't afford to hire an experienced bookkeeper full time, have an employee do the basic data input and then hire a firm or an advanced bookkeeper with a CPA to oversee financials on a monthly basis.

Test Bookkeepers before hiring

If your organization can afford to hire professional help, it's a good idea to put an individual's skills to the test before entrusting them with your financials. A balance sheet and an income statement can be spit out using QuickBooks. If a bookkeeper is able to generate a cash-flow statement, which is required under GAAP, it's a good sign of the level of expertise.

Know how to make Accrual Accounting adjustments

Failing to make accrual accounting adjustments under GAAP, where revenues and expenses are recognized when earned and incurred respectively can affect accounting records. Only recording cash transactions isn't sufficient.

When a nonprofit earns income, for example, this is recorded as a receivable. But often, when a nonprofit receives cash from either grants or program services, it is recorded as revenue.

The journal entry then reflects a debit to cash and credit to revenue, but that's not proper under GAAP. When you receive money from program services or a grant, you're supposed to debit accounts receivable and credit revenue, and that makes a big difference on cutoffs for revenue recognition.

For nonprofits with trained professionals already nonprofit accounting software, such as Intuit's 2014 QuickBooks Premier nonprofit, lets an organization to properly and accurately track their budget against the actual budget expenditures and use certain classes to track funds.

Implement a Review Process

Accounting transactions require a segregation of duties and a review process, meaning all accounting processes should be reviewed by at least two sets of eyes.

8

WHY GRANTS PROPOSALS GET REJECTED

There are few reasons a grant application is rejected. Three of the most important reasons are:

1. The proposal does not follow the application guidelines
2. The nonprofit does not have enough money to approve all grant proposals
3. Your proposal falls outside the target organization's area of interest (your goals don't align with their goals).

How then can you improve your chances of securing funding? You have to improve your grant writing skills.

How to improve grant writing skills

1. Review Application Guidelines

You should read through the guidelines of each grant carefully and ensure that you have (or are able to get) all the materials you'll need to complete your application. Getting your application thrown out because you didn't follow directions is probably the worst way to lose out on funding. It is highly recommend that you create a folder for each grant you plan on applying for so you can easily access your materials and information.

2. Prepare an Outline

Preparing an outline of the elements your proposal will have is quite key to the success of your proposal. It is true that most proposals contain the same information, but you should always check the grant guidelines to see exactly the components to include. The major components of a grant proposal are:

- Letter of Inquiry or Cover Letter
- Executive Summary
- Statement of Need
- Goals and Objectives
- Program Design or Methodology Evaluation
- Project Sustainability
- Nonprofit Organization Information

- Budget.

3. Make a Plan

When you are ready to create the application, you need to plan out how work on the application will proceed. If you are with a group, you could use your outline to delegate each section. Fix due dates for every component and ensure that expectations are crystal clear.

If the application is going to be written by you, ensure to set due dates for yourself so you're not scrambling to finish it in a hurry or at the last minute.

4. Keep it Simple

Although grant proposals are complex documents, trying simple language in your proposal will help the person reading it to spend less time trying to understand your application, and this can motivate them to want to fund it.

Try to write as if you were explaining your organization and goals to a dummy or child. They don't know as much about your organization as you do, so simplicity lets someone unfamiliar with your project to understand it.

Tips for writing simple, readable proposals

- Write conversationally while remaining professional.
- Don't use technical language acronyms or clichés.
- Do not use empty phrases or vague words like about, nearly, almost, or roughly. Always be specific!
- Use charts and graphs to help explain your points.
- Use short paragraphs, headings, and subheadings.

5. Bring in Creativity

A whole lot of grant proposals are boring, but they don't have to! A simple solution is to be creative, tell your organization's story and pinpoint what makes your nonprofit and the project unique. Use creative language to explain exactly how your community would benefit from the funding. Your creativity will go a long way when there are a lot of applicants struggling to grab a limited fund..

6. Proofread Before Sending!

Before your proposal is sent, proofread. Review it for grammar, spelling, syntax, and clarity. Even the smallest errors look bad when you're trying to convince someone to fund a project. In addition, take your time to ensure you've fulfilled all of the application guidelines.

When you've reviewed it yourself, have one of your colleagues do it again. You'll be surprised how they are able to catch mistakes you may have missed.

9

EFFICIENT NONPROFIT ACCOUNTING SOFTWARE

There are lots of great software out there that van help you handle accounting matters for nonprofits. The list below is a personal selection. If none of them suits your organization, you might as well try other software.

1. Abila MIP Advance
2. Abila Fundraising 50
3. Abila MIP Training
4. Accounting Software
5. Abila MIP
6. Admissions Office
7. Blackbaud
8. Nonprofit Accounting Software
9. Fundraising Software
10. Nonprofits
11. Grant Management
12. Nonprofit Software News
13. NetSuite Fund Accounting
14. Raiser's Edge
15. Sage MIP

16. Sage Nonprofit Solutions
17. SerraFund
18. Student Billing
19. MIP Fund Accounting
20. Fund Accounting Software

10

PICTURES OF FINANCIAL STATEMENTS OF NONPROFITS

Example of an Operating Statement: Operating Statement/Statement of Activities for ABC Company for Year Ending 2002**

Changes in Unrestricted Net Assets:	Unrestricted	Temporarily Restricted	Permanently Restricted	Total
Revenues and Gains:				
Public Contributions (net):	$600,000.00	$150,000.00	$30,000.00	$780,000.00
Program Service Revenue:	$50,000.00			$50,000.00
Investment Income:	$30,000.00	$5,000.00		$35,000.00
Net Assets Released from Restrictions:	$100,000.00	$(100,000.00)		$0
Total Revenues, Gains, Other Support:	$780,000.00	$55,000.00	$30,000.00	$865,000.00
Expenses:				
Program Services:	$500,000.00			$500,000.00
General Administration:	$165,000.00			$165,000.00
Fundraising:	$100,000.00			$100,000.00
Total Expenses and Losses:	$765,000.00			$765,000.00
Increase in Net Assets:	$15,000.00	$55,000.00	$30,000.00	$100,000.00
Net Assets as Beginning of Year:	$300,000.00	$0	$500,000.00	$800,000.00
Net Assets as End of Year:	$315,000.00	$55,000.00	$530,000.00	$900,000.00

Cash Flow Worksheet for ABC Nonprofit
10/01/03 to 1/31/04

	October	November	December	January
Opening Cash	500	7,300	5,000	-1,020
Expected Receipts				
Client Fees	250	300	300	300
Meyer Grant	2,000	1,000	1,000	0
Government Grant	1,000	0	0	0
Sales	1,500	2,000	2,000	1,500
Donations	3,000	2,500	2,000	1,500
Other Grants	5,000	3,000	0	0
Receipts Total	12,750	6,300	3,300	3,300
Loans Received	0	0	0	0
Total Cash Available	13,250	13,600	8,330	2,280
Expected Disbursements				
Net Payroll	2,000	3,000	3,200	3,000
Federal Withholding &FICA	700	1,000	1,100	1,000
Sate Withholding	300	500	6,00	500
Workers Compensation	250	400	450	400
Unemployment	250	300	450	400
Health Plan	400	500	800	700
Rent	600	1,200	1,200	1,200
Utilities	250	500	800	700
Office Supplies	200	300	200	100
Insurance	300	400	400	400
Postage	200	300	300	200
Program Supplies	300	400	100	200
Printing	100	100	250	100
Other	100	200	300	0
Loan Repayments	0	0	0	0
Total Disbursements	5,950	7,900	8,950	7,700
Ending Cash	7,300	5,000	-1,020	-6,620

Source: citeseerx.ist.psu.edu

Example of a Performance Based Budget

\multicolumn{5}{c}{Performance Based Budget}				
Performance Area	Type of Activity	Output Measure	Budgeted Output	Total Cost	Avg. Cost
Improve Quality	Change in specific Performance	# of complications	10% reduction	$60,000	6000 per 1 % reduction
Perform Programs	education programs	number of programs	1000	$50,0000	$50/program
Improve Staff Satisfaction	Allow longer breaks and free coffee/donuts	Turnover rate	Reduce turnover by 50% from 6 years To 3 years	$20,000	$10000 /staff member retained

Example of a Flexible Budget:
Flexible Budget for ABC Nonprofit 2004

Volume of Participants per Program		$ 35,000.00	$ 40,000.00	$ 45,000.00
Revenues*				
	Donations	$100,000.00	$100,000.00	$ 100,000.00
	Fees	52,500	60,000	67,500
	Total Revenues	**$187,500.00**	**$200,000.00**	**$ 212,500.00**
Expenses				
	Salaries	$ 50,000.00	$ 50,000.00	$ 50,000.00
	Supplies	70,000	77,000	84,000
	Rent	12,000	12,000	12,000
	Other	5,000	5.000	5,000
	Total Expenses	**$137,000.00**	**$144,000.00**	**$ 151,000.00**
Surplus/(Deficit)		50,500	56,000	661,500

Joseph's House, Inc. (A Non-Profit Organization)
STATEMENTS OF CASH FLOWS
For the Years Ended September 30,

	2013	2012
CASH FLOWS FROM OPERATING ACTIVITIES:		
Increase (decrease) in net assets	$ 43,619	$ (154,590)
Adjustments to reconcile change in net assets to net cash provided by operating activities:		
Depreciation	39,589	30,554
Increase in cash surrender value due to earnings on the policy	(79)	(230)
Decrease (increase) in operating assets:		
Accounts receivable	(2,797)	5,403
Grants receivable	78,758	35,589
Prepaid expenses	(767)	17,610
Increase (decrease) in operating liabilities:		
Accounts payable and employee withholdings	252	3,443
Accrued expenses	(1,217)	(1,632)
Deferred support	(94,676)	(15,550)
Net cash provided (used) by operating activities	62,682	(79,403)
CASH FLOWS USED BY INVESTING ACTIVITIES:		
Purchases of property and equipment	(37,255)	(21,943)
CASH FLOWS FROM FINANCING ACTIVITIES		
Net advance (payment) on capital lease obligation	(936)	3,480
Net advance (payment) on loans and line of credit	-	-
Net cash (used) provided by operating activities	(936)	3,480
NET (DECREASE) INCREASE IN CASH AND CASH EQUIVALENTS	24,491	(97,866)
Cash and cash equivalents, beginning of year	57,466	155,332
Cash and cash equivalents, end of year	$ 81,957	$ 57,466
Interest paid during the year	$ 675	$ 277

Source: josephshouse.org

Joseph's House, Inc. (A Non-Profit Organization)
STATEMENT OF FUNCTIONAL EXPENSES
For the Year Ended September 30, 2012

	Program	Supporting Services			
	Joseph's House	Mgmt & General	Fund-Raising	Total Support	Functional Expenses
Salaries & labor	$ 495,365	$ 43,875	$ 13,404	$ 57,279	$ 552,644
Payroll taxes	38,354	3,409	852	4,261	42,615
Fringe benefits	51,701	4,596	1,149	5,745	57,446
Total payroll related expenses	585,420	51,880	15,405	67,285	652,705
Consultants	21,599	14,240	34,176	48,416	70,015
Legal and accounting	13,378	30,183	16,054	46,237	59,615
Volunteer expenses	52,252	-	-	-	52,252
Meeting and staff costs	44,544	3,231	1,627	4,858	49,402
Insurance	37,851	5,051	2,105	7,156	45,007
Repairs and maintenance	36,937	1,495	-	1,495	38,432
Depreciation	29,026	764	764	1,528	30,554
Food	28,969	-	-	-	28,969
Contracted services	23,063	3,120	-	3,120	26,183
Miscellaneous development	-	-	16,355	16,355	16,355
Utilities	14,225	960	432	1,392	15,617
Household supplies	10,265	-	-	-	10,265
Telephone	9,034	800	244	1,044	10,078
Office supplies	2,276	5,789	-	5,789	8,065
Rent	5,389	599	1,620	2,219	7,608
Transportation	4,507	1,175	-	1,175	5,682
Printing and copying	-	1,116	2,993	4,109	4,109
Postage and delivery	48	1,635	1,651	3,286	3,334
Funeral expenses	836	-	-	-	836
Licenses and permits	-	798	-	798	798
Dues and subscriptions	496	248	-	248	744
Medical supplies	662	-	-	-	662
Program expenses	525	-	-	-	525
Interest	-	277	-	277	277
Miscellaneous expenses	-	1,219	-	1,219	1,219
Totals	$ 921,302	$ 124,580	$ 93,426	$ 218,006	$ 1,139,308

Joseph's House, Inc. (A Non-Profit Organization)
STATEMENT OF ACTIVITIES
For the Year Ended September 30, 2013

	Unrestricted	Temporarily Restricted	Total
SUPPORT & REVENUE:			
Grants and Contributions			
Government grants	$ 429,181	$ -	$ 429,181
Foundation, non-profit and corporate grants	299,000	30,000	329,000
Individual and religious organizations	440,679	-	440,679
Total grants and contributions	1,168,860	30,000	1,198,860
Program service revenue	1,055	-	1,055
Interest income	8	-	8
Increase in cash surrender value	80	-	80
Miscellaneous income	3,010	-	3,010
Net assets releases from restrictions	14,190	(14,190)	-
Total unrestricted support and reclassifications	1,187,203	15,810	1,203,013
EXPENSES:			
Program services			
Joseph House, Inc	966,272	-	966,272
Management and general	114,073	-	114,073
Fundraising	79,049	-	79,049
Net expenses	1,159,394	-	1,159,394
Change in net assets	27,809	15,810	43,619
Net assets, October 1, 2012	695,604	11,250	706,854
Net assets, September 30, 2013	$ 723,413	$ 27,060	$ 750,473

Joseph's House, Inc. (A Non-Profit Organization)
STATEMENTS OF FINANCIAL POSITION
September 30,

	2013	2012
ASSETS		
CURRENT ASSETS:		
Cash and cash equivalents	$ 81,957	$ 57,466
Accounts receivable	3,997	1,200
Grants receivable and promises to give	85,189	163,947
Prepaid expenses	26,193	25,426
Total current assets	197,336	248,039
PROPERTY AND EQUIPMENT:		
Buildings and improvements	1,168,211	1,160,011
Automobile	48,002	23,730
Furniture and fixtures	44,357	40,562
Office equipment	35,689	34,701
Donated equipment	500	500
Household and medical equipment	30,842	30,842
Total property and equipment	1,327,601	1,290,346
Less: accumulated depreciation	715,616	676,027
Property and equipment, net	611,985	614,319
OTHER ASSETS		
Cash Surrender Value	3,561	3,482
TOTAL	$ 812,882	$ 865,840

Joseph's House, Inc. (A Non-Profit Organization)
STATEMENTS OF FINANCIAL POSITION (continued)
September 30,

	2013	2012
CURRENT LIABILITIES:		
Accounts payable and employee withholdings	$ 14,982	$ 14,730
Accrued expenses	44,883	46,100
Capital lease obligation - current portion	775	775
Line of credit	-	-
Deferred support	-	94,676
Total current liabilities	60,640	156,281
LONG-TERM LIABILITIES		
Capital lease obligation	1,769	2,705
NET ASSETS:		
Unrestricted		
Operating	712,836	685,027
Board designated - contingency	10,577	10,577
	723,413	695,604
Temporarily restricted	27,060	11,250
Total net assets	750,473	706,854

11

NONPROFIT ACCOUNTING GLOSSARY

Mission

The reason an organization exists.

Tax exempt

A status granted by the Internal Revenue Service (IRS), granting a nonprofit exemption from federal income taxes. The organization has to meet certain requirements to qualify for this status.

501(c)(3)

Organizations described in Section 501(c)(3) are referred to as charitable organizations and must have charitable, religious, educational or scientific purposes.

Form 1023

IRS Form 1023, Application for Recognition of Exemption Under Section 501(c)(3) of the Internal Revenue Code, is the required form for a nonprofit to file with the IRS to receive its tax-exempt status under 501(c)(3) of the Internal Revenue Code.

Determination letter

Letter received from the IRS by a nonprofit stating that it is tax-exempt from federal income taxes.

Public charity

A nonprofit that generally receives its funding from the general public including individuals, businesses, government, and private foundations.

Private foundation

A nonprofit that generally receives its funding from a single major source.

Generally Accepted Accounting Principles (GAAP)

The standard framework of guidelines for financial accounting established by the Financial Accounting Standards Board (FASB) to ensure that there is accuracy and consistency in financial statements.

Pledge receivable

A promise made by a donor to give a nonprofit a specific sum of money at a particular time.

Conditional promise to give

Promise made by a donor to give a specific sum of money on the basis of a certain criteria. For example, a donor may promise to give an organization $30,000 if the organization first raises $15,000 of other funds.

Contribution

Voluntary donation of funds, services or assets made to a nonprofit in which the donor does not expect to receive anything in return.

In-kind contribution

Contribution of goods or services in lieu of cash.

Net assets

The difference between a nonprofit's total assets and total liabilities. It is similar to a for profit entity's equity. Net assets reveal an organization's net financial worth.

Unrestricted contributions

Contributions to a nonprofit that have no limitations or restrictions as to how they'll be used.

Temporarily restricted contributions

Contribution received by an organization that have been restricted by the donor on what it'll be used for. This restriction is only for a period of time.

Permanently restricted contributions

Contribution received by nonprofit that cannot be spent and must be maintained in perpetuity. The most common examples are endowments that are invested with any earnings available to be spent by the organization.

Board designated

Unrestricted cash received by a nonprofit that has been set aside for a specific purpose by the board of directors.

Program service revenue

Fees and revenue received by a nonprofit for services rendered.

Functional expenses allocation

A method used in dividing expenses between program services, management and general, and fund raising categories using a reasonable, consistent basis. This allocation is required by Generally Accepted Accounting Principles and the IRS.

Program expenses

Expenses necessary in carrying out the mission or purpose of the nonprofit. Examples include; money for food served at a daycare, money for space used for an afterschool program or the salaries of a counselor working with clients.

Management and general expenses

Expenses necessary to keep the organization and its programs running but are not directly connected to a particular program or with fund raising.

Fund raising expenses

Expenses associated with getting donors to contribute to the nonprofit.

Statement of financial position

A required statement in a nonprofit financial statements under GAAP. The statement reveals an organization's assets, liabilities and net assets.

Statement of activities

A required statement that reports a nonprofit's revenues and expenses and the changes in the amounts of each net asset class (unrestricted, temporarily restricted and permanently restricted). .

Form 990

This IRS form must be filed annually by tax-exempt organizations to report information on organization's programs and activities.

Accrued Expense or Liability

Expense or Liability incurred during an accounting period for which payment has not been made (or postponed). Examples include accrued rent payable, accrued salaries, accrued sales tax payable.

Accrued interest

Interest costs that have accumulated, but are yet to be due for payment

Accounts Payable

This refers to the amount owed to others for services or merchandise received by the organization.

Accounts Receivable

This refers to the amount owed to the organization for services or merchandise provided to others. If the amount is related to a grant agreement, it is referred to as Grant Receivable.

Accumulated Depreciation

The total amount all fixed assets have decreased to date as a result of wear and tear or obsolescence.

Allocation

This is actually a method in accounting that divides expenses among different programs, administrating and fundraising categories based on a sharing formula. The formula must recognize the use of resources like facility or staff time.

Amortization

The process of repaying loan principal and interest.

Assumed Name

This refers to an alternative name under which an individual or legal entity can conduct business. it is also called DBA or doing business as a name.

Assets

Properties owned by the organization.

Audit

A financial report that has been verified by a certified accountant in accordance with Generally Accepted Accounting Principles. The accountant is preferably called 'Auditor'. He must write an Opinion Letter about the organization's account.

Balance Sheet

This report shows the assets, Liabilities, and Net assets of the organization. Also called Statement of Financial Position.

ABOUT THE AUTHOR

Tim Jefferson is a Financial Accountant in Florida. He has worked for many for-profit organizations and NGOs in the past seventeen years.

Made in the USA
Monee, IL
15 February 2020